The Rightly-Guided Caliphs

The Rightly-Guided Caliphs

Enis Yüce

New Jersey

14 13 12 11 1 2 3 4

Written by
Enis Yüce

Art Director
Engin Çiftci

Designed by
Nurdoğan Çakmakçı - Ahmet Kahramanoğlu

Published by Tughra Books
345 Clifton Ave., Clifton,
NJ, 07011, USA
www.tughrabooks.com

The Rightly-Guided Caliphs

ISBN: 978-1-59784-261-7

Printed by Çağlayan A.Ş. Izmir, Turkey

TABLE OF CONTENTS

Part 1

A FAITHFUL FRIEND

God Almighty commissioned Prophet Muhammad, peace and blessings be upon him, to teach people the truth and to guide them to the straight path. The Prophet tried very hard to carry out this sacred duty in the best way possible. He thought day and night about the path he should follow to fulfill his duty.

He needed to tell people about God one by one and in secret. The people of evil intentions in Mecca would never let him call people to God's way openly.

The Prophet told his family and close relatives about God's messages first. Some of them accepted the divine truth that the Prophet related to them and embraced Islam. However, they were very few in number. The Prophet wanted all people to learn about the beauty of Islam.

After he explained Islam to his relatives, he decided to talk about it with his close friends. Abu Bakr was the first one among his close friends. Abu Bakr was respected and loved by everyone around him. He would never hurt anyone. He helped those who were in need, and he was a man of mild character, tolerant to others.

The Prophet and Abu Bakr had been close friends for a long time. They used to take walks together and worked together. They always lent each other a hand in times of a trouble.

Abu Bakr had heard some rumors about the Prophet in the city. He heard a man saying,

“They say that Muhammad says it is wrong to worship the idols we believe in. We worship them as our ancestors did. Muhammad is an honest man, but why is he saying such terrible things about our idols?

Some of them were talking even more harshly:

“If he continues to trouble himself with our idols, we will teach him a good lesson.”

Abu Bakr was worried when he heard these conversations. Moreover, he wanted to find out if these rumors were true or not. He wondered what his friend would say about all these rumors.

Abu Bakr decided to visit the Prophet. It had been a long time since he had last seen the Prophet. They missed each other very much. On the same day, the Prophet also decided to see Abu Bakr to tell him about Islam. He was walking toward Abu Bakr's home.

These two friends who missed each other very much met on the road. They did not expect to run into each other like that. They greeted and hugged each other happily.

The Prophet asked Abu Bakr where he was off to.

"I missed you very much Muhammad, I was coming to see you. In fact, I heard some rumors about you from some people. I wanted to ask you about that. They say you are talking about a new religion, is that right?"

The Prophet explained that he had been given the duty of inviting people to God's religion.

Abu Bakr said:

“Would you tell me about this religion?”

The Prophet started to explain Islam. After listening to the Prophet, Abu Bakr said:

“Muhammad, we have been friends for years. I never witnessed anything bad you did or said. I never heard you tell a lie. I believe that what you are telling me about is true.” And then he asked:

“I believe in the religion you are sharing with me. How can I join in this religion?”

The Prophet became very happy and excited, and he taught him the shahadah, the proclamation of faith. And then Abu Bakr became a Muslim.

The Prophet was very happy. He hugged his friend and said:

“You should not tell anyone about this right now.”

He knew that the Meccans would not like to hear that Abu Bakr had become a Muslim.

Days passed and Islam was spreading quietly. The number of Muslims had increased to thirty-eight. Abu Bakr was learning new things about Islam every day, and he was so happy. But he felt so sad to see people around him doing evil things to each other.

"Islam aims to eliminate all the harms on Earth. I wish all people became Muslims so that all troubles of the world would perish," Abu Bakr said to himself.

Seeing that the number of Muslims was increasing very slowly, he was impatient sometimes and once said to the Prophet:

"O Messenger of God! Why don't we call people to Islam openly rather than in secret?"

The Prophet answered him that the number of believers was very few and they did not have enough strength to do that.

Abu Bakr thought the Prophet was right after listening to what he said.

However, one day, Abu Bakr came to see the Prophet and asked for his permission to call people to Islam openly. And he insisted on this.

The Messenger of God accepted this finally.

The Prophet and his friends went to a crowded place in Mecca. Abu Bakr stood up on a high place where people could see him and started talking. He told people that idols cannot benefit them, and that God is one and the only deity. He invited them to believe in God and His Mes-

senger. When unbelievers saw Abu Bakr talking about a new religion, they attacked the Prophet and his friends.

While Abu Bakr was telling people about what he knew about Islam, a group of people pulled him down and began to beat him. They kicked him on the ground. Abu Bakr was bleeding badly.

In the meantime, Abu Bakr's relatives learned what happened. They came and saved him from unbelievers' hands. He was very exhausted. Every part of his body became swollen and purple from the beating he received. There was blood all over his head and face. It seemed to people that he was going to die. They took him to his mother's house. They tried very hard to get him to come round. However, Abu Bakr remained unconscious; he could not even open his eyes. Hours passed after the event, but he still could not speak a word. He opened his eyes in the evening at last. The people there were so happy to see this.

"Thank God! He has finally come around!"

"Yes, look at his eyes. He moved them slightly," they said.

His friends were watching him anxiously. His lips were moving, but he could not speak. It was evident that he wanted to say something.

Everyone waited silently to hear what he was going to say. He might want water or something to eat. However Abu Bakr's first words really surprised everyone:

"How is the Messenger of God?"

These were his first words after he regained his consciousness. The people who were gathered around him could not believe their ears.

Abu Bakr was not thinking about his own bad situation, but rather he was wondering whether his friend was okay. The people told him:

"You are in bad shape. You almost died. Every part of your body is wounded. Moreover, you were beaten because you were with him. You should care about yourself, but you are asking how well the Prophet is?"

It was no doubt that the people around him could not understand his special love for him. Abu Bakr and the Prophet were very close friends. There was a special bond between them. Moreover, one of them was a prophet now, and Abu Bakr had also a great respect for the Prophet as well as a deep love.

Seeing that Abu Bakr was no longer at risk of death, his relatives left his home. Finally, he was alone with his elderly mother. When he was

feeling much better, he asked his mother the same question. "Has anything happened to the Messenger of God? Do you know how he is now?

"I do not know anything about his situation," she answered.

"Then can you go and find out for me how he is doing?"

"But you are not feeling well; you just came round. You may need some help, how can I leave you alone here?"

"Do not worry about me. I need to know how he is right away."

His mother understood that she was not going to be able to convince Abu Bakr, so she left to ask about the Prophet's relatives about his condition.

She was walking in the streets of Mecca uneasily. She was worried about her wounded son at home.

She went up to the house of one of the Prophet's relatives. She knocked at the door.

"Who is it?" someone asked.

"It's me, Abu Bakr's mother," she replied.

The owner of the house let her come in. Abu Bakr's mother immediately started talking, as she did not want to lose time:

"My son is badly wounded. But he asked about Muhammad's situation as soon as he opened his eyes. If you know about Muhammad's situation, can you please let me know so that I can tell my son?"

The woman who opened the door had become a Muslim before, and she knew Abu Bakr and that he was a Muslim, too. But she was cautious about giving information about the Prophet; the enemies could attempt to harm him. She answered her:

"I'll come with you. I want to inform him myself."

Abu Bakr's mother did not think about it for long. They went to Abu Bakr's home together. They walked very fast and finally got there.

When they opened the door, the woman could not believe her eyes. She said:

"May God punish those who did this to you!"

She expressed her sorrow for him and wished him quick recovery. Abu Bakr, however, was not thinking about himself. He asked the woman inquisitively:

"How is the Prophet? Has anything happened to him?"

"Thanks to God Almighty, his situation is fine now.

"Where is he now?"

The woman pointed at Abu Bakr's mother and said:

"I do not want to talk about him in front of her." Abu Bakr said:

"Do not worry. She is my mother. She will not do anything that may put him in danger. She will not say anything to anyone."

Then she said where he was recovering, "He is staying at his friend's house."

Abu Bakr asked her to take him to where the Prophet was.

Meanwhile, Abu Bakr's mother was busy making soup for her son. When she heard that he wanted to see the Prophet she said:

"My son, you are not in a good condition. How can you go there? Have some soup first. You can go when you feel better."

However Abu Bakr was very anxious about the Prophet's condition. He wanted to make sure that he was really fine.

He told his mother:

"I will not eat anything before I see my friend."

His mother saw how determined he was and agreed to take him to where the Prophet was. All three of them left home. Abu Bakr was walking with great difficulty. They brought him to where the Prophet was staying. They knocked at the door. One of the Prophet's Companions opened the door. The people in the house were so surprised to see Abu Bakr there.

His face was swollen and bruised, he could hardly stand up. Abu Bakr looked very bad. But he was still worried about the Prophet. When he got into the room, the Prophet saw his faithful friend's condition, too. He stood up and hugged him. He was so sad to see him in that condition.

Abu Bakr's mind was finally at peace seeing that the Prophet was fine. It was as if his wounds were no longer hurting him. He pointed to his mother and said to the Prophet:

"O Messenger of God, could you please pray to God for my mother to become a Muslim. I want it so much."

Abu Bakr's mother had already understood what a beautiful religion Islam was. His son became such a wonderful person after being a Muslim. It was very touching for his mother to see her son's love for the Prophet, too.

The Prophet prayed to God opening his hands toward the sky. Then Abu Bakr's mother said the words of *shahadah* there and became a Muslim.

After that they asked for the Prophet's permission to leave. Abu Bakr was feeling much better now. His friend was in good condition and his dear mother was now a Muslim. They went home with the feelings of gratefulness to God.

A COMPANION FOR THE JOURNEY

The Prophet was with his close friend Abu Bakr. He said hesitantly:

"O Messenger of God! Unbelievers are giving Muslims a hard time every day. There are not many Muslims left in Mecca. If you give me permission, I would like to immigrate to Medina, too."

The Prophet told Abu Bakr to wait until God gives him permission to leave so that they might emigrate together.

Abu Bakr was delighted to hear that the Prophet had chosen him as his company during his journey. He bought two camels that day and started to feed them for their journey.

Unbelievers in Mecca continued to persecute Muslims. Unable to resist the persecution, Muslims were immigrating to Medina in small groups. Both Muslims from Medina and the Muslims who had immigrated there invited the Prophet to Medina.

The Prophet learned that unbelievers had made a plan to assassinate him. He started making preparations for the journey. When he was ready to go, he left his home to go to his friend Abu Bakr's house.

"Abu Bakr, God gave me permission to emigrate. Get ready for the journey," the Prophet said.

"O Messenger of God, I have been feeding two camels for the journey for a long time. Let me bring them here," said Abu Bakr.

The Prophet was surprised to hear that. He didn't know about the camels.

"I can accept the camels only if I pay their price," he said.

Abu Bakr did not want to accept this offer at first, but the Prophet was so insistent that he had to agree.

Abu Bakr's family loved the Prophet very much, too. Abu Bakr's daughter Asma prepared food for them to eat during the journey.

Abu Bakr gave his son Abdullah an important task. Abdullah would spy on the unbelievers to learn their plans. Then he would convey the information to Abu Bakr and to the Prophet.

After Abu Bakr and the Messenger of God had finished their preparations, they checked if there was anyone outside. Making sure it was safe outside, they left home quietly.

When they set off for the journey, the unbelievers of Mecca went to the Prophet's house to kill him. When they did not find him home, they thought that he could have gone to his close friend Abu Bakr's house. They went there and started knocking at the door loudly.

Asma, Abu Bakr's daughter opened the door fearfully. Unbelievers were waiting in front of the door with swords in their hands. They asked:

"Is Muhammad here?"

"No," replied Asma.

"Is Abu Bakr here?" they asked.

"No," replied Asma again.

They got very angry and started slapping Asma. They pushed her into the house. They searched for every single place in the house to find them. But they found neither the Prophet nor his faithful friend Abu Bakr. They left home angrily. They looked for them far and wide in Mecca.

After leaving home, the Prophet and Abu Bakr were going to Medina according to the way they had planned before. They did not choose the

known and common way to go to Medina. They were going to Medina over the Thawr Mountain.

After a long way, they came in front of the Thawr Cave. The cave was very quiet. It was very scary.

Abu Bakr got into the cave first thinking that there might be some insects and spiders that might hurt the Prophet. He looked all over the place. Then he cleaned a spot in the cave. There were some snake and scorpion holes around. He took off his shirt and tore it into pieces to close the holes. But his shirt was not sufficient to close all the holes. One of them stayed open.

They were both very tired; they had not taken a single break. Abu Bakr sat on the ground. The Prophet put his head on his lap and lay on the ground in order to get some rest.

Abu Bakr placed his foot on the hole that he could not close with his shirt. He was worried. A dangerous animal like a scorpion or a snake could go out from there and give harm to the Prophet. He wanted to prevent animals from going out from that hole by his foot.

Although Abu Bakr was very tired, he could not sleep. Trusting Abu Bakr, the Prophet fell asleep. Abu Bakr felt a terrible pain in his foot at that moment. He moved his foot a little bit, and he saw a snake's head there. The snake was trying to get out from the hole where Abu Bakr put his foot as all the other holes were closed.

This snake knew that the Prophet had come to this cave, and he tried every other hole to get out and see him. At the end he had to bite Abu Bakr's foot in order to see the Prophet.

The bite was very painful for Abu Bakr. He wanted to scream, but he did not as he thought it would disturb the Prophet. It was so painful that tears started to fall down from his eyes. One of the drops touched the face of the Messenger of God.

The Prophet woke up when he felt the drop on his face. He asked Abu Bakr:

"What happened? Why are you crying?"

"A snake bit me, O Messenger of God," said Abu Bakr.

The Prophet was so sad to see his faithful friend in pain. He prayed to God to relieve his friend's pain. He touched his hand to Abu Bakr's foot, and it was cured.

After they got into the cave a pigeon started to make a nest in front

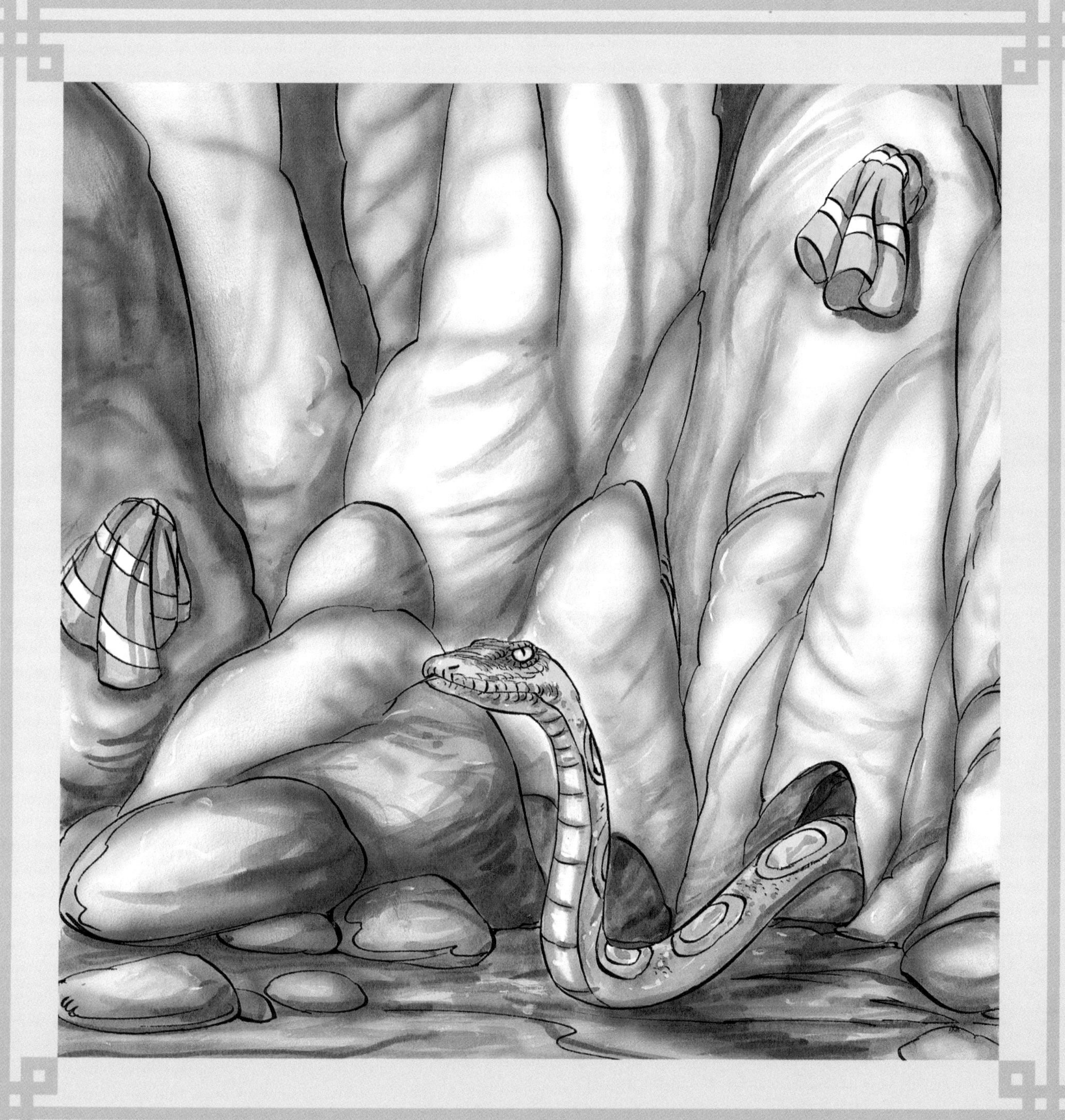

of the entrance of the cave. This pigeon was hastily carrying straws to build the nest.

Meanwhile a spider was also making a web at the entrance of the cave. This spider was working very hard and fast. In a very short time its web covered the entrance of the cave.

Unbelievers could not find the Prophet in Mecca, so they assigned groups of men to go and find him. One of the groups searched the way between Abu Bakr's house and the desert. As they noticed the footprints on the desert, they started to follow them. They were hopeful to find them now. The footprints led them to the cave. One of them said,

"We have finally found them. Look here! There are no more footprints forward."

They all looked at the footprints carefully. The footprints ended in front of the cave. They went to the entrance of the cave excitedly. One of them cried:

"Then they must be still here. They cannot escape from us any longer."

The Messenger of God and Abu Bakr could hear them from inside. The Prophet asked Abu Bakr:

“Are you afraid?”

“O Messenger of God. May my mother and my father be sacrificed for your sake! I am not worried about myself; I am worried about you. I am only one of the servants of God. However you are both a servant and the Messenger of God,” answered Abu Bakr.

“Do not worry Abu Bakr; God is with us!” said the Prophet.

Meanwhile one of the unbelievers said:

“I will go inside and check.”

The others were waiting at the entrance. Just as he was going into the cave, one of them said:

“Do not go in vain. We should not waste our time here. Do you not see? A pigeon had made a nest here. If there were anyone in the cave, the pigeon would not stay here.”

Another one said:

“I am sure that they are not here. Look at this spider’s web! The cave’s entrance is covered by the web. It takes several weeks for a spider to make such a big web. We should not waste our time by going inside the cave. We should go further to find them.”

The others saw the pigeon's net and the spider's web and thought their friends were right. In fact, the spider had started making this huge web that morning and finished it in a very short time. They did not realize that. All of them left the entrance of the cave.

None of the groups of unbelievers could find the Prophet and Abu Bakr that day. They got very angry. They held another meeting right away.

One of them said:

"They could not have gone so far away. We should find them."

Another one said:

"The best thing to do is to give a big reward to the person who will bring us their heads."

"We give a hundred camels to the person who will find them," someone said.

Owning a hundred camels was great wealth at that time. They decided to let all Meccans know about this new plan. After that, town criers walked in the streets of Mecca and let everyone know about this offer. Whoever could bring Muhammad dead or alive would be rewarded by a hundred camels.

Some of the unbelievers were more eager to find him when they heard the reward.

One of them was a man named Suraqa, who was a strong man who could use sword and ride a horse very well. To have a hundred camels was something he dreamed of.

"I will find and bring them before everyone else. I will take the prize and become rich," he thought.

He got prepared quickly and set out. He was riding his horse very fast without caring about the heat of the desert. The dream of having a hundred camels didn't leave his mind. As he rode his horse through the desert, he saw two people ahead of him. "Those two must be them," he thought. He rode faster when he saw them. He was moving like the wind. He came very close to them. He made sure that these two people were the Prophet and his faithful friend Abu Bakr.

Abu Bakr got very worried as he saw Suraqa behind them. The Prophet was calm, however. When he saw that Abu Bakr was anxious, he repeated what he said to him in the cave:

"Do not worry, Abu Bakr. God is with us!"

After that the Prophet turned his face to Suraqa and looked at him.

At that point, Suraqa's horse's feet sank into the sand, and the horse was no longer able to move further. Suraqa tried to take his horse's feet out of the sand, and he managed this after a big effort.

He started to ride his horse again. However, his horse's feet sank into the sand again. And this time, Suraqa was not able to move his horse a single step.

Finally, he understood that he couldn't catch the Prophet no matter how much he tried. Although he was very strong and a good swordsman, he could not do anything with his might.

He got off his horse and walked up to the Prophet and Abu Bakr, leaving his horse stuck in the sand. He turned to the Prophet and apologized to him:

"O Muhammad, I understand that what just happened to me and my horse is because of you and your special duty. I am sorry for what I did. Please pray to your God so that I can save my horse. I will not harm you. I will go back and mislead those who have been chasing you."

The Prophet understood Suraqa's regret from his eyes. He prayed to God and his horse was saved from the sand. Suraqa got on his horse and left them immediately.

On his way back, Suraqa met some others who were chasing the Prophet and Abu Bakr to kill. He said to them:

"I am coming from this way; they are not there."

And then they changed their way.

Unbelievers of Mecca failed once again. The city of Medina was waiting to welcome the Prophet.

THE MONEY SAVED IN THE CLAY POT

After the Prophet passed away, Muslims chose Abu Bakr as the head of the state. His friends congratulated him on his new position. They prayed to God to be his helper.

The following morning, people got up early and were getting ready for work. The sun was rising. The sellers were trying to prepare their goods to take them to the bazaar. Everybody was in a hurry.

Caliph Abu Bakr got up early that day as usual. He went to the stable to milk the cows. He put the milk into the buckets. After that he left home to go to the bazaar.

On his way, he heard someone calling behind him:

"Where are you going Abu Bakr?"

He recognized this strong voice right away. It was his best friend Umar's voice. He turned and saw Umar approaching him. Umar asked the same question once again with a surprised expression on his face:

"Where are you going?"

Actually, Umar understood where he was going to since the road Abu Bakr was taking was the way of bazaar.

Abu Bakr answered him calmly:

"I am going to the bazaar."

Umar thought that he was going to the bazaar as caliph to make sure everything was going all right. However, he still asked to make sure:

"What are you going to do there?"

"I am going to do what I usually do."

"What do you mean? Are you going to sell something in the bazaar?

"Yes, I am."

"But you are the caliph of all Muslims; you are the head of the state. You should be taking care of the business of the state."

"But I have a family and children. I need to sell these goods in the bazaar to support them. I need to continue the job I was doing before I became the caliph."

"Of course, you need to support your family," said Umar.

"How can I do this then if I stop working?"asked Abu Bakr.

After thinking over Abu Bakr's words, Umar said:

"You go now. I will talk to some friends, and I will suggest that you be given a salary from the treasury of the state."

Abu Bakr did not want to take salary from the state.

"No, I cannot accept a salary from the state. I think that it is more appropriate if I support my family with the money I earn myself," he said.

Umar said:

"I will talk to my friends and then let you know the results."

After considering Abu Bakr's situation carefully, Umar decided to talk to his friends about it. He invited his friends to his home to discuss the issue. They came to Umar's home after a while. They were wondering what he wanted to talk to them about and what urgent matter could have made them meet so early in the morning.

The meeting was about to start. Everyone was looking for Caliph Abu Bakr. But he was not there.

Umar took the floor first:

"I want to talk to you about an issue regarding the caliph. That's why I invited you here."

One of his friends said:

"We chose him as the caliph yesterday, and we are all done with this. What more is there to discuss in this matter?"

Umar continued his words:

"I saw him this morning. He was going to the bazaar as he did before. I want him to deal with the needs and problems of the public. He needs to spend all his time on the business of the state. He should not do trade in the bazaar. He is the head of the state now."

One of the people in the meeting asked:

"How can he earn money to support his family then? How can he earn money if he does not work?"

Umar answered:

"I suggest that he be given a salary from the treasury of the state. This is why I called you to come here this morning."

Some of the people there said:

"What a good idea! We never thought about this before. It is true that he needs to spend all his time working for the state, and a salary should be given to him."

After they discussed it all together, they decided that he should be given enough salary with which an average person could support his family. One of the people in the meeting was Abu Ubayda who was the treasurer of the state. Umar told Abu Ubayda:

"Let's give Abu Bakr's first salary together. After that, you will give it to him."

Abu Ubayda accepted this. Meanwhile, Abu Bakr reached the bazaar to sell his goods, which he did after some time.

He bought some groceries for his family and left the bazaar to go home.

When he arrived home, he saw Umar and Abu Ubayda waiting for him in front of his house. He greeted them.

Umar greeted him too and he said

"Let's go."

“Where are we going?” asked Abu Bakr.

“We will give you a salary from the treasury, said Umar.

“But I do not want salary. I can sleep less at night and work harder during the day. I can support my family with the money I earn from the bazaar. I don’t want to take salary from the state.” Umar insisted:

“Abu Bakr, this is not my own idea. This is a decision we made all together. You should spend your time dealing with the needs of the Muslims. The state should give you a salary in return.”

At first, Abu Bakr did not accept their decision. However, Umar insisted firmly. As a result of his friend’s hard insistence, he accepted the offer.

According to the decision of the committee, Umar and Abu Ubayda gave him a monthly salary of three hundred and fifty dirhams.

This amount of money was enough for a regular person to get by on those days. It was much less than the amount of money the rich earned monthly.

Abu Bakr was busy with the business of the state until midnight from then on. He would listen to people’s complaints and help them. As he worked during the night, he started to go to bed later than he did before. He would also get up very early every day.

In his free time, he herded camels as he did before being the caliph. Everybody was astounded to see him like that.

It had been two years since Abu Bakr became the caliph.

He worked very hard for two years standing on his dignity. One day, he was going home at a very late hour after a long day of work. He was not feeling well that night. He thought he was just tired. He thought he was going to be okay if he had some rest. He went home and went to bed right away.

He felt worse when he got up in the morning. His family members did not leave his side. However, he wanted to go and take care of his work as soon as possible.

Abu Bakr straightened himself up in the bed with great difficulty. He felt that he would die soon. He called his son, who was taking care of him. He told him about a clay jar, the location of which no one else knew. He asked him to bring that jar to him. Then he put a letter that he had written before into the jar and covered it.

Abu Bakr gave the jar to his son and said to him:

"O son, take this jar. There is a letter in the jar for the next caliph. Give the jar and the letter to the person that is going to be caliph after me."

His son took the jar with tears in his eyes.

"Certainly, my dear father," he said.

Abu Bakr's sickness became worse, and he died soon thereafter. Umar was elected as the next caliph. Abu Bakr's son took the jar that his father had given to him and gave it to Umar. He said to him:

"My father wanted me to give this trust to you. There is a letter inside of it that is for you."

Umar tried to open the jar. As he could not open it, he broke it. It was full of golden coins. He found the letter among the coins.

The letter read like this:

"These are the salaries I took from the state. I spent some of it. I saved the rest in this jar. This money belongs to the treasury of the state."

Umar read the letter with tears in his eyes. He said:

"Abu Bakr set a great example and lived a life that is very hard for us to live."

He was crying silently.

Part 2

UMAR FINDS THE TRUE PATH

It was the hottest time of year in Mecca. People were sick of the heat and preferred to stay inside their homes. There were just a few men on the empty streets. A few men who looked angry went into a house with quick steps.

A man waiting in front of the door took them inside then he went out again. He saw a very strong man coming toward him. He turned to the people inside and said:

"Umar is coming, too!"

After Umar came in, they closed the door and started talking to each other. The people gathered in this house were the richest and most powerful people in Mecca. The common point that brought them together was their fear and anger.

They heard that Prophet Muhammad was teaching a new religion to the people around him. They were really concerned because so many people had believed in him in such a short time. Actually, they had known him since he was a child. They all knew that he was a very reliable and honest person. But what the Prophet Muhammad had been telling people recently made them very angry.

One of them said:

"We have to take immediate action. It wouldn't be so important if he was the only person who believed in what he said. But in a very short period of time, a lot of people have gathered around him. They believe in the things he has been telling them."

Another one said angrily:

"They say he tells them that believing in our idols and our ancestors' beliefs are all wrong."

Another one sitting next to him said:

"It is said that he tells people 'God sent me a holy book.' People reading and listening to that book are very impressed, they say. It is written in this book that all people are equal. Can you imagine that our

slaves and we are equal? If the number of people following Muhammad increases, we won't be able to find anybody to serve us."

One of them, dressed elegantly said:

"Well my dear friends, all of this shows that there is only one thing that can be done. We need to get rid of him before the danger grows."

"Yes, you are right. There is no other way to stop this without killing him."

"But who is going to kill him? The people following him love him so much that they would easily sacrifice their own lives for him. So the person who is going to kill him should be prepared to deal with the people around him, too."

One of them stood up and said:

"The only person that could overcome this hard task is Umar."

The others looked at Umar and said:

"Yes Umar, such a job can be done only by a person who is as courageous as you."

With these words in praise of him, they were trying to encourage Umar to kill the Prophet. Under the influence of what had been told to him, Umar put on his sword and set out. He made his decision. He would kill the Prophet at all costs. He was very angry and nervous.

He came across met a man called Nuaym on his way. When Nuaym saw Umar walking hurriedly, he called out:

"Where are you off to?"

After giving him a fierce look, Umar said:

"To kill Muhammad."

"Why?"

"Because I heard that he has been diverting people from believing in our idols with his new religion. He tells them that he is a prophet, and the people have been gathering around him. The number of the people who believe in him is increasing day by day."

Nuaym was shocked by his words. He loved the Prophet very much too and didn't want him to get hurt. He thought he could change Umar's mind, but Umar was very angry and determined not to be convinced by him. At least he wanted to gain some time to let the Prophet know about the situation. In order to keep him busy, he needed to divert his attention to somewhere else. He said to Umar:

"What you heard is true. But let me tell you something that is going to make you much more annoyed. I have heard that your sister and her husband joined them and became Muslims, too. I think you would rather talk to them first before you kill Muhammad."

Umar couldn't believe what he heard.

"I don't believe you! You made this up!"

"If you don't believe me, then go and ask them," said Nuaym.

"I am going now. But if you have lied to me, you will be sorry for this," said Umar and walked away immediately. He changed his mind and decided to go to his sister's home. While he was on his way, he couldn't stop thinking 'What if the Nuaym was telling the truth…' If his friends heard that his sister had become a Muslim, what would his friends say about him?

He didn't even see the people around him because of his anger. He walked very fast to reach to his sister's house. There were some voices coming from the house. His sister Fatima, her husband Said bin Amr and Habbab, one of the Muslims, were at home. They were reciting the Qur'an. Umar tried to understand those voices. He got close to the window. He could hear the voices better now. It was not like a regular conversation.

“It must be the book that came to Muhammad,” he said to himself.

He could not understand it exactly, but the things they were reading were really different and interesting.

He approached to the door and started to knock forcefully. From the way his was knocking, the people inside the home understood that Umar was at the door. Habbab hid somewhere in the house right away. His sister and her husband wanted to hide the pages of the verses of the Qur’an because they knew that Umar would be very angry with them. Fatima panicked and said:

“Let’s hide them at once. If Umar sees them, he will get very angry with us.”

They hid the verses. In the meantime, Umar kept pounding at the door yelling:

“It’s Umar, open the door right away!”

Fatima, Umar’s sister, opened the door with fear. Umar entered the house and approached his brother-in-law and asked:

“Did you convert? Did you accept the religion that Muhammad brought?”

KNOCK!
KNOCK!

His brother-in-law understood that Umar had heard what they had been reading. When he said, "Maybe the religion we chose is better than yours," Umar became very angry and started to kick him. When Umar's sister tried to break them up, he slapped her and knocked her down. Fatima's lip started to bleed.

She stood up and cried to Umar furiously:

"Look Umar, it is not right to believe in idols as you do. The true faith is what the Prophet brought us from God Almighty."

When Umar saw that his sister and her husband were unyielding, he kept hurting them. Finally, he understood that whatever he did would not make them give up their new religion. Suddenly, he remembered the words he had heard when he was outside. He said to Fatima:

"What were you reading? Show it to me."

His sister and brother-in-law looked at each other in surprise. Then Fatima took out the papers from where they hid and handed them to Umar. The Sura of Taha was written on the papers. Umar started to read the verses. After he read a little bit, he calmed down and felt peace deep in his heart. Then he said:

"These words are different. They are not like any poems or anything written by a human being."

He seemed impressed by the verses he had read. His sister and her husband couldn't believe what they heard. Umar's attitude had totally changed, and he was reading the Qur'an calmly. After he finished reading, he said:

"Take me to Muhammad!"

His brother-in-law asked worriedly:

"Why do you want to see Muhammad? Are you going to hurt him?"

"I wanted to kill him until I came here. Just a few minutes ago, after reading the pages you gave me, I want to listen to what he is saying," replied Umar.

Habbab ibn Arat who had been watching everything from where he had hidden became very excited when he heard Umar's words. Umar was very surprised because he didn't know that Habbab was there. He had heard that Habbab had become a Muslim, too. He thought he could learn something about Islam from him, so he asked him:

"Tell me about the religion Muhammad brought."

Habbab started to tell about Islam. It was obvious that Umar was impressed. After a while he said to Habbab:

"I would also like to embrace your faith. Just take me to Muhammad."

"Congratulations Umar! You have found the true path. The Prophet's prayers are answered now. He always prayed to God for you to become a Muslim," said Habbab excitedly.

Umar was excited. The feelings he had before coming to his sister's home were totally different than what he was feeling at this moment. He was full of anger before, but now he felt peace inside. He turned to Habbab and said:

"Please take me to him!"

"Okay, let's go right now!" said Habbab happily.

They all set out to Prophet Muhammad's home. When they got close to his home, the Prophet's friends saw them and became very worried.

They informed the Prophet and asked him what to do.

"Allow him to come inside," said the Prophet.

The Prophet's friends agreed, but they were still worried and couldn't stop thinking, "What if Umar has a bad intention..."

One of the prominent Muslims, Hamzah said:

“Don’t worry! If Umar has come here with good intention, he’s welcome. Otherwise, I am going to kill him with my own sword.”

After that the door was opened. Habbab and Umar came inside the house and greeted everybody. The Prophet and his friends greeted him, too. Umar approached the Prophet and sat in front of him and said that he would like to become a Muslim. The Prophet and Umar said the *shahadah* together.

The Prophet and his friends were very happy. Umar ibn al-Khattab was one of the strongest, bravest, and most influential people in Mecca. He was so strong that he would even wrestle with camels. The believers would be much stronger than before with Umar on their side. That’s why, Prophet Muhammad had prayed a lot for Umar to become a Muslim. He was so grateful to God Almighty for accepting his prayers. Everybody there congratulated Umar. The number of the Muslims increased to forty with Umar. Umar wanted to tell everybody about Islam. He said to the Prophet:

“O Messenger of God, why don’t we invite people to Islam openly? People should immediately learn about such an excellent religion.”

Then he got permission from the Prophet to visit the Kabah. The meaning of the Kabah was very different to him now. He was walking around the Kabah repeating *shadahah* aloud. The people who heard this immediately informed Abu Jahl, the enemy of the Muslims.

"Alas! Umar joined them, too. Muhammad is more powerful now," they said.

Abu Jahl couldn't believe what he heard because he knew that Umar set out to kill Muhammad just a few hours ago.

"How do you know this?" he asked them.

"If you don't believe us, go and see him for yourself. He's at the Kabah. Abu Jahl stood up in a hurry.

He went straight to the Kabah. He saw Umar coming from the Kabah. He approached him and said:

"I heard that you changed your religion. Is that right?"

"Yes, that's right. I believe that there is no deity but God and Muhammad is the Messenger of God," said Umar.

Abu Jahl and his friends were shocked when they heard that Umar had converted to Islam because a very influential person in Mecca had abandoned them and joined the Prophet's community.

Umar became an outstanding person with his intelligence, courage, power, and justice. After a short time, he became one of the best friends of the Prophet.

THE BOILING STONES

After the Prophet passed away, the country was ruled by his closest Companion, Abu Bakr. After Abu Bakr's death, Umar became the ruler of the country. Umar was very a close friend of both the Prophet and Abu Bakr.

After the Prophet's death, the rulers of the country were referred as caliphs. When Umar became the caliph, the borders of the country extended far and wide. Thus Umar's duties were also much greater in number than before. He was working very hard day and night to solve people's problems.

One day, after a tiring day as usual, he was returning home with his assistant Aslam.

"It is too cold tonight, isn't it, sir? asked Aslam.

"Yes, it's very cold," replied Umar.

Just then, he noticed a light of fire burning far away from them.

"Aslam, do you see that fire?"

"Yes, I see it, sir."

"Who could have made that fire?"

"I don't know, sir."

"There may be people who are cold out there. Or maybe, they are some travelers who stopped over because of the dark and cold weather. They might need help.

"Yes, sir."

"Let's go there, then."

They started to walk toward the burning fire, which was a long distance away. They were talking to each other as they were walking. It was late at night, and the streets were almost empty. People had already gone home and were getting ready to go to bed. Umar and Aslam, on the other hand, were walking into that cold night. They looked happy although they were cold because they were going to help people in need.

When they got very close to the fire, the scene they saw shocked them. They hadn't expected such a thing.

There were an old lady and children crying next to the fire. On the fire was a pan with water in it. The children were watching the boiling pan. They frequently opened the lid of the pan to look inside it.

The lady and children didn't know Umar and Aslam. They were both surprised and a bit scared to see them. Umar asked her:

"Can we come closer?"

"Come if you will help solve my problem"

The lady did not understand that the person she was talking to was Caliph Umar, the leader of the Muslims. In fact, she didn't know him at all, so it was impossible for her to recognize him. Moreover, Umar always dressed like an ordinary person, and his attitude was not different from others.

Umar asked curiously:

"What's going on here?"

"We are homeless. I am trying to keep my children warm with this fire."

"Why are your children crying?"

"Because they are hungry. I couldn't find any food for them."

“But what is the thing boiling in this pan? Isn’t it food?”

The lady opened the lid of the pan and showed them what was in it. Then she told them what she had done.

“I put some stones in the pan with some water because we have no food. I have been stirring the water with a ladle so that I can keep my kids busy. I hope that they fall a sleep after a while. I can do nothing else to stop them crying because they are very hungry.”

After the lady told them her story, she continued:

“It’s for sure that Caliph Umar will be called to account by God Almighty for this!”

Umar was suddenly taken aback by her words and asked:

“How could Umar possibly be aware of your situation?”

The old lady answered with a pathetic voice:

“If he didn’t know, how did he become a caliph to rule the country?”

Umar was appalled by her answer. Then he left with Aslam right away. The woman was very surprised by what had happened: Two strangers had come, listened to her, and then left without saying anything.

Umar and Aslam started to walk to the food storehouse of the city. Umar was still under the influence of the old woman's last words. He was walking with fast steps. Aslam was having a hard time keeping up with him. Finally, they arrived at the food storehouse. They filled a sack with food for the woman and her children.

Aslam understood what was Umar was thinking and wanted to carry the sack.

But Umar did not allow him:

"No, Aslam. I have to carry this myself."

"How could this be, sir? I am your servant. I can't let you carry that sack," he insisted.

Umar said with a determined voice:

"Give me a hand to put this sack on my back."

"But how can I do this? Please let me carry it!"

"I am responsible for those people. I am supposed to solve their problems. Put this sack on my back and you take the oil bottle," he said.

The great caliph walked all the way to the woman's place with a heavy sack on his back in such a cold weather at night.

When they arrived there, the scene was the same as before. The children were still awake. The expression on the old woman's face was even sadder. She was stirring the water with a ladle saying:

"Umar will be held responsible for this on the Day of Judgment."

That Umar and Aslam came back surprised the old woman and her children. They wondered who those people coming in the middle of the night could be?

Aslam helped Umar put the sack full of food on the ground. The fire under the pan was about to fade away. Umar asked for permission from the woman and started to blow the fire to rekindle it.

Aslam put some wood that he collected on the fire. Umar kept blowing the fire. Then he took some food out of the sack to prepare a meal. He was trying to prepare the food as quickly as possible. After a short time, the meal was ready.

Umar and Aslam served the food to the family as soon as it was cooked. Umar knew that the children wouldn't wait for the food to get cool. He put some food in the plates. However, they were too shy to eat. So he held their hands and brought them to the food. He also invited the

woman. They were very hungry. Umar kept serving food in their plates until they were full.

After a while children were full and started to play games. The woman was very happy to see that her children were not crying anymore. She thought and said to herself "How could I have fed my children if these people hadn't come? I'm so grateful to them."

The lady turned to Umar and said:

"You should be our caliph instead of Umar."

"Why?" asked Umar.

"Because he doesn't know how hard his people's lives are and doesn't help the poor. But you helped us although you didn't know who we are."

Hearing this Umar said:

"You should go to see Umar tomorrow and explain your situation. He may give you a child care allowance so that your children won't suffer from the poverty anymore."

In the meantime, the children fell asleep near the fire with full stomachs. Umar and his assistant were very happy fulfilling their duty. The woman thanked them and prayed for them a lot as they were leaving.

The old woman thought about what the stranger had advised her to do and decided to go to see Umar in the morning.

The following day, she went to talk to Umar, who she had never seen before. While she was on her way, she was wondering whether or not the caliph would accept her request. She was still worried when she arrived at the caliph's house. She asked where the caliph's room was. She knocked on the door and entered the room. She was very surprised by who she saw in the room. It was the caliph himself who brought a heavy sack of food on his back and cooked for them the night before.

Umar stood up to welcome the old woman. He asked why she was in such a bad situation. He felt very sorry for her, so he provided a maintenance allowance for her family.

THE WATCHMAN OF THE CARAVAN

The sun was about to set. The weather was cool, and the wind was blowing. There was a cloud of dust going toward Medina. The cloud of dust was caused by a long caravan passing through the desert.

A lot of camels and horses loaded with goods were moving in a row. The owners of the goods were walking by their animals. They were go-

ing to sell their goods that they were bringing from far away cities to make money.

It was getting dark. The caravan had been on its way for a few days. The camels, horses, and people were all exhausted. Everybody wanted to find a secure place where they could stop to rest for the night.

An old man was leading the caravan. He was going to decide when the caravan could stop because this man knew the trade routes very well.

When the caravan approached Medina, people started asking to each other:

"When are we going to stop and take a break?"

Everybody looked at the old man. He looked very tired too, but he didn't want to show his tiredness as he was the leader of the caravan.

After a while, they saw a free plain near Medina.

The man leading the caravan said:

"We can stop and rest here! All of us are very tired. We are going to have a rest tonight. We can continue our way in the morning."

Everybody was very happy. They couldn't sleep well for days because of the long and tiring trip. They prepared to sleep right away. Some

of them still had worries about the city. They didn't know what sort of people lived in the city. Were they going to be safe during the night?

They gathered around the leader of the caravan. The old man was thinking about how to continue the journey and was making plans. One of them asked to the old man:

"Everybody is very tired. We don't have energy even to stand up. What if we are attacked during the night?"

The leader of the caravan was worried too. After he listened to him, he said:

"Yes, I don't know this area either." He pointed to city sparkling lights and said:

"But as far as I know, the people of the city are Muslims. I have heard that Muslims are reliable people."

Another man around the caravan leader interrupted:

"I also heard about their trustworthiness, too. But we are Christians. They might treat us badly because we follow a different religion. Moreover, this place is a route through which other caravans and other people pass. They might hurt us."

After listening to their ideas, the leader of the caravan gave his opinion:

"Yes, we need to be prudent. We can place watchmen during the night. When we sleep, they can keep an eye on our caravan."

Then he called six young men from the caravan and said:

"You are the strongest people in the caravan. Tonight, we are camping by a route where other caravans are passing through. While we are asleep, some evil-minded people might hurt us and our animals. So you are going to be up tonight to protect us, our watchmen."

These young men were also very tired, but after their caravan leader talked to them, they said:

"All right! Don't worry. You can sleep in peace. We are going to watch the caravan."

Shortly after the watchmen began their duties, the others went to bed and fell asleep right away.

The six young men watching the caravan were divided into three groups. They were walking around the caravan. After a few hours, they lost their energy to stay awake, because they had been traveling for many days like the others. So eventually, they fell asleep, too.

There was nobody awake to watch the caravan anymore after the watchmen fell asleep.

After a short time, somebody approached the caravan. He walked around the caravan a few times. He checked whether there were any watchmen or not. This person was Umar. He always walked out to make sure that there was nothing causing a nuisance for the people in the streets of Medina at midnight.

He went out to walk around the streets that night, too. While he was walking, he noticed the caravan camping near the city. Then he decided to go to see the caravan. He couldn't see anybody up. Everybody was sleeping. He walked around the caravan several times to see if someone was awake. He wanted to learn who they were, where they were coming from, and whether or not they needed anything.

He could tell that they were Christians.

He was the head of the state. But he was working day and night to make sure that not only Muslims but also the non-Muslims living in his country were happy.

He thought that he was also responsible for the security of these people. But he had nothing to protect them with at that time. He knew his people; Muslims wouldn't hurt them.

However, the place where caravan was camping was a very busy route which was used by many different people. Their precious goods could be stolen in such a place where no watchmen existed.

After considering all these things, he made a decision. He went to his close friend Abdurrahman's house and knocked on the door hastily.

Abdurrahman, waking up in the middle of the night, was worried. Who could be knocking on the door at such a late hour?

He rushed to the door. He was even more surprised when he saw Umar at his door. Umar first greeted him.

"Assalamu Alaikum, Abdurrahman!"

"wa Alaikum Salaam. Please come in! I hope everything is all right."

"No, thank you. Get ready! We need to go somewhere."

"Where are we going?"

"There is a caravan camping near the city. They are all sleeping. There is nobody guarding them."

"Where are they coming from and where are they going?"

"I don't know, Abdurrahman. They were all asleep. Looking at their

property, I suppose that they are Christians. I am worried about them. They might get hurt. Get ready! Let's go there to guard the caravan."

"Ok, I am coming, sir."

They left the house right away. They were walking very fast as they thought that thieves might hurt the travelers. Finally, they arrived at where the caravan was camping.

They didn't wake anybody up, assuming they were exhausted. They went up to a hill next to the caravan where they could keep watch easily. They weren't sleepy.

While they were watching out for them, the six young men chosen as watchmen were still sleeping. After a while, one of those young men woke up and looked around. He saw that his friends were sleeping, too. He was still sleepy. He thought that everybody was sleeping, so he could sleep too. Just then he saw Umar and Abdurrahman near the caravan. He was confused. He couldn't understand if it was a dream or not. He was so tired that he didn't even have the energy to stand up. Although he didn't want to sleep, he couldn't keep his eyes open. But after a while he woke up once again with anxiety. He thought those two people could be thieves who came to steal their goods. He looked at

property, I suppose that they are Christians. I am worried about them. They might get hurt. Get ready! Let's go there to guard the caravan."

"Ok, I am coming, sir."

They left the house right away. They were walking very fast as they thought that thieves might hurt the travelers. Finally, they arrived at where the caravan was camping.

They didn't wake anybody up, assuming they were exhausted. They went up to a hill next to the caravan where they could keep watch easily. They weren't sleepy.

While they were watching out for them, the six young men chosen as watchmen were still sleeping. After a while, one of those young men woke up and looked around. He saw that his friends were sleeping, too. He was still sleepy. He thought that everybody was sleeping, so he could sleep too. Just then he saw Umar and Abdurrahman near the caravan. He was confused. He couldn't understand if it was a dream or not. He was so tired that he didn't even have the energy to stand up. Although he didn't want to sleep, he couldn't keep his eyes open. But after a while he woke up once again with anxiety. He thought those two people could be thieves who came to steal their goods. He looked at

them carefully to make sure he wasn't dreaming. He had no doubt that there were two men waiting; it wasn't a dream.

He kept watching them for a while. They weren't stealing anything. He said to himself, "If they were bad people, they could have robbed us while everybody was sleeping. Our leader must have paid for them to guard our caravan." He thought of waking up the leader to ask him about those two men. But then he changed his mind.

"There is no need to warn the leader of the caravan. Everybody will wake up soon anyway. I'll ask them when they wake up. I'd better sleep a little more before the sunrise. Tomorrow, we will have another long trip. I should sleep," he thought.

In the meantime, Umar and Abdurrahman were chatting and keeping their eyes on caravan.

It was very early in the morning; the sun was about to reveal its first rays soon. People in the caravan started to wake up. The caravan leader woke up, too. When they saw they were getting up, Caliph Umar and his friend Abdurrahman got ready to go to the morning prayer. Umar said:

"The sun will rise soon. They have started to wake up, so they don't need us anymore. Let's go to the city for the morning prayer." They shook the dust off their clothes and headed for the city.

At that time, the young man went to talk to his caravan leader. He told him about what he had seen during the night.

"Did you hire the two men watching for the caravan last night?"

The leader had no idea what he was talking about.

"Who are you talking about?" he asked.

"I am talking about the two strangers who watched over our caravan last night."

The leader was very surprised.

"No, I didn't assign anybody but you."

The young man thought he had made a big mistake. Then those people must have been thieves if they hadn't been watchmen. He couldn't keep himself awake, and he couldn't catch them. He was worried and said:

"Then they were thieves and stole all our precious things when the watchmen were asleep."

Upon hearing this, the caravan leader became very worried, too. He told everybody to check their own belongings and to report if anything

was missing. They all checked their property, but there was nothing missing.

So those two mysterious people weren't thieves. The caravan leader said:

"They must have come here to watch and protect us if they weren't thieves."

Then he turned to young man and said:

"Would you recognize them if you saw them again?"

"Yes, I would. When I saw them, I was sleepy, but I remember their faces."

"They couldn't have gone far away. Go find them and learn who they are and why they watched over our caravan."

The young man left immediately to find in which direction the two strangers went. Then he saw two people going toward the city. Those must be the two strangers, he thought. He followed them secretly.

Meanwhile, everybody in the caravan woke up. The leader told them what the young man had told him. They were very curious, too.

Who were those men? Why did they watch the caravan for them? Nobody could come up with an answer.

Umar and Abdurrahman arrived at the city. The young man following them asked the people he met on his way who they were.

The first man he asked said:

"How come you don't know them? He is our caliph Umar and the man next to him is one of his close friends, Abdurrahman ibn Awf."

Young man couldn't believe what he heard.

"This man is probably making fun of me. A ruler of a country would never do such a thing instead of sleeping in his lovely bed at night," he thought.

He asked several other people the same question, and he got the same answer. The young man was convinced. He rushed back to the caravan. He went up to the caravan leader right away. Everybody was still talking about what happened last night.

The leader of the caravan asked him curiously:

"Were you able to learn who those men watching for us were?"

"Yes, I was. But you won't believe me."

Everybody became even more curious with his answer.

"Those who were guarding us were Umar, the leader of Muslims, and his close friend, Abdurrahman."

Everybody was silent for a while. Especially the leader of caravan was quite surprised. He traveled a lot and had heard about Umar almost everywhere he had visited.

"How could that be possible? Umar, who conquered many countries and is the leader of all Muslims, was a watchman for the people with whom he doesn't even share the same belief," he said.

It was an incredible event for them. After a minute of silence, the caravan leader gathered them around him and said:

"My dear friends! I think that Umar's exceptional conduct is because of his religion. What a beautiful religion is Islam. I would like to go to find Umar, and then I am going to choose Islam as my religion."

Then he headed to Medina to find Umar. People seeing their leader go said:

"We also want to become Muslims." They joined him. After a while, they found Umar and talked to him about their decision. Then they embraced Islam.

Part 3

GOOD NEWS

The sun was setting, and the Meccans were returning to their homes after work. Uthman closed his shop and was going his home as the others. He was very tired that day. As he took off his shoes to go into his home, he heard some familiar voices coming from inside the house. His mother and his aunt were talking to each other. He heard his aunt say:

"I am very sure that he says the truth. He is a very honest man."

But he did not know about whom they were talking. Since they were talking about honesty, he thought that they might have been talking about a tradesman. When Uthman opened the door and went into the house, his aunt and his mother stopped speaking immediately. They

did not hear him coming as they were much immersed in their conversation. They looked a little worried and looked into each other's eyes. It seemed as if they were hiding something from Uthman. He greeted his aunt and kissed her hands and hugged her. He loved his aunt very much. He sat in front of them and asked:

"Who were you talking about when I came in?"

They were talking about the Prophet; he had declared that he was the Messenger of God. The people of Mecca had reacted in different ways to this new call of Muhammad, peace and blessings be upon him. While a few people accepted this call, many of them did not welcome this new occurrence.

Since Uthman's mother and aunt did not know how Uthman would respond to this, they hesitated to talk to him about it. However, Uthman insisted on learning who they were talking about. His mother and aunt did not want to answer. This made Uthman even more curious to know. He repeated his question. At last, his aunt decided to tell him who they were talking about:

"Muhammad is saying that he has been appointed messenger by God. We were talking about this. We did not want to tell you as we feared you would get angry with us."

Uthman said, "Why would I get angry with you? I heard about it, too. I am mystified; however, I have never heard him tell a lie before."

His aunt said, "We have known Muhammad for a very long time. Everyone knows for sure that he is a very trustworthy person. No one ever has heard a lie from his mouth. He has never told a lie even to make jokes. Why on earth should he tell a lie on this matter? How can such a person tell a lie concerning God? Who can tell a lie saying God appointed him as His messenger?"

"It is true. We all know that he never lies, and he is trustworthy. Do you know what else he talks about?" Uthman asked.

"He says that people should be kind to others, respect their parents, and be honest. He also prohibits abusing the rights of orphans," his aunt replied.

"However, he rejects worshipping our idols and does not want people to seek help from them," said Uthman.

"I think it makes sense, too. Tell me Uthman, can those lifeless idols help even themselves? Then how can they help people? Do not we make them with our own hands? I heard that there are some women who accepted Islam. I may go and tell the Prophet that I will accept Islam.

You also should think about his call. If your heart says that he is telling the truth, you should go and support him in his way," his aunt said.

Time passed very fast as they were talking. Uthman's aunt asked to leave to go home. Uthman and his mother said goodbye to her.

Uthman was very confused after their talk. He went to his room early that night. He said to himself, "Muhammad is an honest man. He never tells lies. But if he is telling the truth then everything we have been doing to worship our idols was worthless and meaningless. He thought over and over about what he had talked with his aunt about. He could not fall asleep although it was very late at night. After thinking for a long time, he decided that he should talk to some close friends of the Prophet. Whom could he talk to? After some time, he decided to speak with Abu Bakr. He was the Prophet's best friend, and he knew him best. He wanted to talk to him immediately, but it was very late at night. He could not disturb him at that time of the night. He wished for morning to come very quickly so that he could find Abu Bakr and speak to him.

After a long night, the beams of the sun started to show up in his room. He was very excited. He decided not to go to work that morning; he would find Abu Bakr and talk to him.

Since he knew that some notables of Mecca were watching the Prophet and his friends closely, he thought that he should talk to Abu Bakr in secret. He left his home and was approaching Abu Bakr's house. While he was walking, he was watching around to see if anyone was following him. He was in front of Abu Bakr's house. He knocked at the door.

Abu Bakr opened the door. He was not expecting to see Uthman. He said to him,

"Welcome Uthman, do you have something to say?"

Uthman said, "I want to talk to you about your friend Muhammad."

Abu Bakr got a bit anxious when he heard the name of the Prophet. He was worried that the unbelievers might have harmed him.

"Has something happened to him?" asked Abu Bakr worriedly.

"No! Don't worry, nothing has happened to him. I just want to talk about the religion that he is inviting people to."

Abu Bakr took a deep sigh. Then he looked around; he was worried that some unbelievers might have been watching them. He told Uthman to come into his house.

Uthman asked Abu Bakr every question he had. Abu Bakr answered all his questions, and his answers were very convincing to Uthman. When

they were deep in their conversation, someone knocked at the door. Abu Bakr went to open the door and turned around with a smiling face. Uthman was about to ask who had come, but he saw the Prophet walking behind Abu Bakr. The Prophet greeted him. Since Uthman decided to become a Muslim after his talk with Abu Bakr, he was very happy to see the Prophet there. He did not want to lose any more time, and he wanted to become a Muslim as soon as possible. The Prophet told him:

"I invite you to accept that there is no deity other than God and I am His messenger. And he taught him how to say the words of the Shahadah. Uthman stood up, held the Prophet's hands and hugged him. He embraced Islam by saying "Ash-hadu an la ilaha illa Allah wa ash-hadu anna Muhammadan abduhu wa rasuluhu" (I bear witness that there is no god but Allah, and that Muhammad is His servant and Messenger).

The Prophet and Abu Bakr were so happy for all this. Uthman promised the Prophet that he would be with him all the time and would support him in his way. After that he asked their permission to leave. Uthman was in high spirits when he left. He walked very fast and arrived at his aunt's house. He wanted to tell his aunt the good news as soon as possible. He knocked at the door, and his aunt opened it. His aunt hadn't seen Uthman so happy and excited in a long time. She was just going to ask what happened, but Uthman hugged her very fast and told her immediately:

"I am coming from where I met the Messenger of God. I accepted Islam, and I promised to support him on his way." His aunt was very happy when she heard that. Uthman's uncle passed by at that moment and heard everything they said.

Uthman's uncle did not like the Prophet. When he heard that his nephew had become a Muslim, he got very angry. He left without their knowing and took some other people with him. They seized Uthman and tied him to a pillar. They whipped him, trying to force him to change his mind about Islam and to worship idols again. Uthman said:

"I am a Muslim, and I will only worship God from now on. I will never change my mind!"

Although his uncle tried hard, he was not able to change Uthman's mind about Islam. He untied Uthman and freed him. Uthman was tortured on the first day he became a Muslim. He was so grateful for getting to know the Prophet and becoming a Muslim despite everything. He would never leave his faith no matter what happened.

THE WELL

Medina was experiencing lively days; Meccans were emigrating from Mecca to Medina regularly.

Muslims in Mecca were undergoing great troubles there because of the unbeliever's persecution and suppression on them. Their life was getting harder and harder in Mecca, so Muslims who got permission from the Prophet started to emigrate from Mecca to Medina in small groups, leaving all their properties back in Mecca.

After all Muslims immigrated to Medina, the Prophet also came to Medina with his best friend Abu Bakr. Muslims in Medina welcomed them with great joy. Everyone was in the streets singing religious songs for him. The first thing the Prophet declared to them was that Muslims from Mecca and Muslims in Medina were brothers and sisters.

Muslims in Medina were called "Ansar" (Helpers) and the Muslims from Mecca were called "Muhajirun" (Emigrants). Every one of the Muhajirun was going to stay in the home of an Ansar. The Ansar helped their new brothers and sisters as much as they could. They shared their houses, their food, and everything they had. The Muhajirun were very happy.

They no longer had to face the torture of unbelievers, and they were with their Ansar brothers and sisters who were helping them very much.

They started to build new houses for themselves in Medina after a time. In order to make a living, some of the Muhajirun worked in fields or in date gardens with the Ansar. Some of them sold goods in Medina's bazaars, and some worked as porters.

The Muhajirun got used to living in Medina. They started to feel like home in there. The Muhajirun kids loved their friends. They soon settled down in this new city completely. However, there was a problem that made life difficult for the Muhajirun: drought.

The Muhajirun had abundant Zam Zam water in Mecca. However, water in Medina did not taste good. They found it hard to get used to drinking this water. Even when they were very thirsty, they could drink only a little water. It was very hard to survive without water in the hot days of the summer in Medina.

This situation affected the children most. As they were playing outside all day long, they got very thirsty and could not quench their thirst with the water of Medina they drank. The hot days of summer were very hard for them.

Actually, there was water that tasted very good in Medina. One of the Ansar had a well in his garden that had delicious water in it. The landowner had spent so much effort digging this well, and he finally found a delicious spring. Since he had no other income, he made his living selling this water to people. The ones who had money came to his garden to buy water.

The Muhajirun who brought some money with them when they left Mecca were able to buy this water. However, most of the Muhajirun did not have money with them as they had left all their property back in Mecca. That is why only a few of the Muhajirun could buy this water. Medinans tried to make their guests comfortable and bought this water for them. They offered this delicious water to the Muhajirun even before having it themselves. But they were not able to do this all the time. Most of them lived a simple life; they were not rich people, either.

The Prophet used to sit and talk with the Muhajirun and Ansar almost every day after the daily prayers in the mosque. He taught them about Islam. They asked the Prophet what they did not know and told him about their problems. One day, the Prophet was having a talk with

his friends. He asked them about their needs and problems as he always did. One of the Muhajirun stood up and said:

"O Messenger of God! Thanks God that we have a comfortable life here. We were saved from the tortures we faced in Mecca. Our Ansar friends are very kind and helpful to us. They share everything they have with us." After saying this, he continued his words by saying, "We are happy about everything. However, we haven't been able to get used to drinking Medina's water."

Another man added, "There is a delicious water spring coming out of a well. However, the owner of the well sells this water. If we had money, we could buy water from him. But we no longer have enough money to buy water from him."

Another man took floor saying:

"We can handle this as grownups. But our children are taking it very hard. They cannot drink water from any other place but from that well.

After listening to his friends, the Prophet started to think of a solution. He never wanted Muslims to suffer. He knew the hardships his friends were going through very well. He had come from Mecca just as his friends had before him. He was not able to trade in the market place as he did in Mecca. That is why he did not have so much money with him, either. If he'd had enough money, he would have bought the well, and Muslims could have drunk from the delicious water of the well for free.

The Prophet decided to talk to the owner of the well. When he arrived at his home, the owner was taking water out of the well. The man looked very tired, but when he saw the Prophet he ran to welcome him. The Prophet greeted him. The man was so happy.

"Welcome, O Messenger of God," he said.

The Prophet told him about the problem of the Muhajirun not having good water. When finishing his explaining, he said to him,

"If you donate this well for the use of Muslims, God will surely reward you for this in Paradise."

The man was surprised. He was speaking to the loveliest person on Earth, with the Prophet. He would even sacrifice his life for something he wanted. The Prophet was asking him to donate his well. He lowered his head.

"I wish I were rich!" he said to himself. If he were rich, he would give the well without thinking much. But if he could no longer earn

money from the well, how could he support his family? He had no income other than this well. He did not have a garden or a field. He raised his head slowly and said:

"O Messenger of God! I really feel so bad for the situation of my brothers. However, I have no property to bring me money other than this well. I am supporting my family with the money I earn from this well." He stopped for a moment and then continued:

"Please give me some time to think about this."

After hearing this, The Prophet thought the man was right, and he left.

The water problem was getting worse day by day. One of the best friends of the Prophet, Uthman was feeling very sorry about this. Uthman was a very rich person when he was in Mecca, and he solved many of the Muslims' problems there easily. He had dozens of camels and caravans of goods. But when he emigrated from Mecca, he had left all his fields, gardens, and goods there. He brought only a certain amount of money with himself as everyone else. He was spending this money for his Muslim brothers and sisters as well as himself, and it was almost gone.

However, he felt uneasy about the Muslims' water problem. He could not even sleep thinking about it.

One morning, he left his home thoughtfully. He was going to see the Prophet. He went to his home and knocked at his door. The Prophet was not home. Uthman decided to go to the mosque. It was the place the Prophet generally used to be when he was not home. When Uthman arrived at the mosque, he saw some of his friends having a conversation. He greeted them and asked if they had seen the Prophet. They told him that the Prophet had gone to talk with the owner of the well for the second time. Uthman felt much more concerned since he understood how much the Prophet was bothered with the water problem.

Uthman could bear anything but to see the Prophet unhappy. He went home and took all his money. He headed to the garden where the well was. He found the owner of the well there. He greeted him and said:

"How are you? I heard that the Prophet came to see you."

The man knew Uthman. He answered:

"Yes, he was here just a minute ago."

"What did he want from you?" asked Uthman.

"He wanted me to grant the well to the Muslims. He said if I did this, God would reward me in Paradise," the owner of the well replied.

"What did you say?"

"I wanted some more time from him to think about this since I have no other income to support my family."

"Would you sell this well to me?" Uthman asked him.

"Yes. I would sell it if someone can pay me its price."

"How much money do you sell it for?"

"Thirty five thousand dirhams."

"If I give this amount of money, would you sell it to me?"

"Sure."

Uthman counted all the money he brought. It was exactly thirty five thousand dirhams. He gave it to the man.

The man was surprised. He was not expecting this to happen that fast. He took the money and said:

"This well is yours, Uthman."

Uthman had no money left. But he did not even care about that. He left the well as fast as he could and looked for the Prophet. Finally, he learned that the Prophet was helping a Muslim and his friends build his house. Uthman walked to where they were.

His friends thought that there was a problem when they saw Uthman coming very fast. Uthman came and greeted them. Then he turned to the Prophet and said:

"O Messenger of God! I heard that you said the one who will grant the well to the Muslims would be rewarded in Paradise? Is that true?"

"Yes, that's true indeed," said the Prophet.

"Then our Muslim brothers and sisters may use the well for free. I have bought the well and donated it for the use of the Muslims," Uthman said.

After hearing this, the Prophet and his Companions were very much touched, and their eyes were filled with tears. The good news spread all around Medina very fast, and everyone was very happy.

THE TRUE CUSTOMER

"It has not rained for months."

"No, unfortunately, it hasn't."

Everyone was saying these words every day. Many months had passed without a drop of rain in Medina. People were very unhappy.

They were looking at the sky with a hope of rain everyday. They sometimes saw some small black clouds in the sky and became excited by the hope of rain.

But those clouds brought no rain. Those awaiting rain went home desperately.

The plants in the gardens of Medina turned pale, and the wheat dried in the fields before they produced spikes. Even little children were aware of the problem, and they were not as cheerful as they used to be. They felt sad seeing their parents unhappy. The abundant food they had before was running out day by day. Green grass on which they played turned yellow and dried up.

Animals were also affected by the drought. They no longer had green grass to eat and did not have access to enough water to drink. Lambs did not run as they used to do; they'd lost their joy like the children.

People were trying to find enough food to satisfy their hunger. Even though everyone was living under such harsh conditions, they tried to help the ones who were in worse a situation than themselves. They shared whatever they had with others: bread or wheat.

During this time of drought, Abu Bakr was the Caliph of Muslims.

He knew the problems of his people as the head of the state and he tried to find solutions for them. He tried to help the people as much as he could.

However, since it had not rained, the wheat did not grow. The storehouses of the state were empty. Since the amount of wheat in the hands of the tradesmen was decreasing everyday, the price of it was increasing continuously.

Some people wanted to use this troublesome situation to their own advantage. Some tradesmen did not sell the wheat in their hands and waited for the price to go up higher. They wanted to gain more profit. If there was any wheat coming into the city, these tradesmen bought it first and then sold it for a very high price. Those tradesmen were not Muslims.

People asked them:

"Don't you see that people are experiencing hard times? Why do you sell the wheat for a very high price?"

They answered them cunningly:

"What can we do? We buy it at a very high price, too."

The drought never seemed to come to an end. The distress in peoples' hearts doubled with the heat of the weather. The possibility of starvation was increasing everyday.

However, one day there was good news spreading around Medina. People were telling each other:

"Did you hear that Uthman's wheat caravan is coming from Damascus? Uthman will sell the wheat at a cheaper price. It will make life a lot easier for us."

In a very short time, all the people in Medina learned about the news. The tradesmen heard that Uthman is coming with a wheat caravan.

It was sure that the wheat Uthman was bringing would be sold at a lower price. Uthman always helped people whenever they were in trouble. The tradesman knew this and feared that they would not be able to sell their wheat at high prices any longer. Therefore, they came together to make a plan.

One of them said:

"If Uthman sells the wheat at a lower price in Medina, it will decrease our profit. We need to do something."

Another one said:

"But what can we do?"

The one who took the floor first proposed his plan:

“Before Uthman comes to Medina, we should meet him and buy all the wheat he is bringing.”

One of them said:

“OK, I understand. We should buy Uthman’s wheat by paying its price. After that, we can sell it at a higher price. People will have to accept the price we ask in order not to starve.”

They all agreed with this plan. They mounted their horses to meet Uthman before it was too late. They wanted to buy all the wheat before the caravan of wheat reached Medina and was sold to anyone. On the road, they were all thinking about how much money they would gain from that business. After they went a long way, they reached the way that caravans passed through. After waiting for sometime, they saw a caravan coming towards them. One of them shouted:

“Look over there; they are coming!”

Another one said:

“Let’s wait a little longer, be patient; it may not be Uthman’s caravan.”

After the caravan came closer, they understood for sure that it was Uthman's caravan. They felt happy and thought that they had arrived in time.

When the caravan was close enough to them, they rode their horses to the caravan and stopped the caravan. Uthman was in the front of the caravan. The tradesmen came closer to him. Uthman was very surprised. He wondered why these tradesmen stopped his caravan.

One of the tradesmen greeted him:

"Where are you coming from Uthman?"

"We are coming from Damascus," Uthman replied.

"It seems that you made a good trade. What are your camels carrying?" he asked.

"I am bringing wheat to Medina," said Uthman.

Another tradesman said impatiently:

"Uthman, we want to buy all the wheat you are bringing. You do not have to carry it to Medina all the way. Let's make an agreement here, sell it to us, and we will take it to Medina."

Uthman said, "No, I am not thinking of selling my wheat to you."

Another tradesman broke in:

"Tell us how much you want for it. We will pay you whatever you want."

And then he offered Uthman a very good price since he thought they could sell it to a much higher price.

However, Uthman was determined not to sell.

"I do not want to sell my wheat to you because someone else will pay a higher price," he said.

Those men of greed were surprised to hear that. They were worried that they were going to lose all the profit they were planning to earn. They continued to insist, offering more money each time.

Every time they increased their price, Uthman said that there was someone who would pay a higher price.

This answer angered them. When they understood that they were not going to convince him, they opened the way for the caravan. As the caravan was leaving, they talked among themselves.

"Sure. He knows that people are in a very hard condition. He must be thinking of selling his wheat at a higher price to them."

Their plan did not work and they were trying to thinkwhat else they could do. One of them came up with an idea:

"Let's complain about him to the Caliph. He may have to sell the wheat to us after that."

"What? Complain about him to the Caliph? But what can we say about him?"

"We should say that Uthman is keeping his wheat so that he can sell it for a higher price."

They liked this idea. They all agreed and went to see the Caliph. When Caliph Abu Bakr saw them anxious, he asked them:

"What happened? Do you have something to say to me?"

The most cunning one among them said:

"We are tradesmen. We buy goods in bulk and sell them in small amounts. This is the way we make our living. We heard that Uthman brought some wheat from Damascus. We went to buy wheat from him, but he did not sell it to us."

Abu Bakr asked, "Why wouldn't he sell?

"You know, since the drought, the price of the wheat has been

increasing every day. We assume that Uthman is waiting for the price to go much higher to sell his wheat. It seems that his intention is to make much more money. You are the Caliph of Muslims who can prevent this from happening. When everyone is in a miserable condition, you should not let tradesmen keep their wheat to sell it for a higher price later."

"Uthman is not that sort person you are talking about; he would never do such a thing," Abu Bakr said after listening to them.

The tradesmen said immediately:

"We may go and talk to Uthman together, if you like. You may convince him."

Abu Bakr agreed:

"All right, I am coming with you. I want to hear the other side of the story from Uthman, too."

The tradesmen took the Caliph Abu Bakr with them and went to see Uthman. At that time, Uthman had just reached Medina with his caravan. As he passed through with his caravan, people were watching them.

Caliph Abu Bakr and the tradesmen went up to Uthman and greeted him. Uthman returned their greetings, and he hugged Abu Bakr. He understood that the tradesmen had complained about him to Abu Bakr.

Abu Bakr said to him:

"Uthman, you know what hard times people are going through these days. We have been in the middle of a drought for a long time. These tradesmen, as I heard, came to buy your wheat, but you did not sell your wheat to them. They are your customers. You have always sold the goods you bring from other countries to Medina. Why won't you sell your wheat to them although they were ready to give you a good price?"

Uthman kept silent for a moment and then said:

"Yes, Abu Bakr! I live in this city, and I know the hard situation of people very well. That is why I did not sell my wheat."

Caliph Abu Bakr and the tradesmen were all surprised. Abu Bakr asked:

"What do you mean Uthman?"

Uthman smiled and continued his words:

"I will not sell my wheat because people may not even have the money to buy it. I want to give half of my wheat away to Muslims for free. Moreover, my true customers are not these greedy tradesmen but people who are in a desperate situation and helpless.

The One who gives a higher price for this wheat is God. That is why I will give it for free for the sake of God.

Abu Bakr understood Uthman's intention and said:

"I see, Uthman. I knew you wouldn't do something wrong."

Uthman did as he promised the following day. He had seen this kind of behavior from the Prophet. He made announcements that he would give wheat to people in need for free. He gave away tons of wheat.

The people in need were so happy that they received help in such a hard time. For Uthman, to see people pleased was much more beautiful than making money.

Part 4

THE YOUNG HERO

The city of Mecca was experiencing tough times. The relationships between people were getting worse every day. People were treating each other badly for their own advantage. Rich people did not help poor people anymore; on the contrary, they looked down on them. Salesmen in the marketplace often told lies to sell their products. Everybody was cheating on each other and was trying to seize each others' property.

In such a tough time, the Prophet declared that he was the Messenger of God. He started to invite all people to Islam, to a life of morality and honesty. He told people that injustice was bad and that it was bad to tell lies. He talked about the countless benefits of following God's orders.

After a short time, the Prophet started telling them about Islam, and some changes began to take place in Mecca. People who listened to the Prophet became Muslims one by one.

The people who became Muslims gave up doing any injustices and bad deeds. However, this situation started to disturb the people who did not believe in God because they thought that they wouldn't be able to do whatever they wanted anymore if the number of good people increased. So they didn't want the number of Muslims to increase.

There were not many Muslims in Mecca yet, so they were not very influential. Polytheists often insulted and harmed Muslims. Despite all the difficulties they had to face, Muslims held onto their religion with great patience. They never gave up following the Prophet.

The religion of Islam conveyed by the Prophet began to spread in other cities as well. The people coming from other towns and cities would come to listen to the Prophet and some of them became Muslims. Many people came from the city of Medina and met the Prophet.

The people who learned Islam from the Prophet related what they learned to other people in Medina. As a result, the number of Muslims was increasing day by day.

Meanwhile, the oppression of disbelievers toward Muslims was getting worse each day in Mecca. Because of this, Muslims were experiencing very tough days.

One day Muslims in Medina sent a message to the Prophet and invited him and other Muslims to Medina. On one of the really tough days, God allowed the Prophet to travel to Medina. Muslims would be able to move to a place where they could live their religion freely.

After the Prophet conveyed the message of God to Muslims, a heart-wrenching emigration from Mecca began. Muslims started to leave the city where they were born and grew up to worship God freely. They left their houses, property, fields, and everything they had behind.

They set off toward Medina in order to live the religion of Islam openly and freely. The Muslims in Medina welcomed them even while they were still on the way. They put them up in their houses and shared everything they had.

That Muslims immigrated and started to settle in Medina disturbed the polytheists in Mecca. They were worried that the Muslims might grow stronger and take revenge from them.

One day they gathered to discuss this issue.

"Have you heard the news? The people of Medina have treated those who emigrated from Mecca so kindly!" one of them said.

"Yes, that's true. If it goes on like that, the number of Muslims will increase much more!" someone responded.

Another man stood up angrily and said:

"It is said that Muhammad is going to emigrate, too. That's the real danger. If he goes to Medina too, a lot of people will probably gather around him as in Mecca. If their number increases, it will be very difficult to deal with them."

The others agreed with his opinion.

"Yes, he is right."

They were all afraid of Islam spreading out. Abu Jahl, one of the leaders of the polytheists of Mecca took the floor:

"The best solution is to prevent him from going to Medina."

One of them asked doubtfully, "But how?"

"We will either kill or imprison him!" said Abu Jahl smiling sneakily.

There was a disagreement among the polytheists. They were divided into two camps. What would be better - to kill or to imprison him? They discussed it for a long time. Finally, Abu Jahl said:

"It's better to kill him, so that we can get rid of him for good!"

One of them stood up and asked:

"You are right but no matter who kills Muhammad, one thing is for sure - his family and followers will try to take revenge. What can we do about this?"

Abu Jahl was a devious man. He looked at the people around him and said:

"We are going to choose one man from each tribe who is very good at using sword. And then they are going to surround Muhammad's house. When he leaves his house, those men will attack him immediately. They are going to kill him altogether so that no one will know who killed him. His family will never be able to find out who the murderer was.

Everybody in the meeting thought it was a perfect plan. So they started the preparations without delay.

In the meantime, the Prophet learned about the polytheists' meeting and their plan. He knew that his house would be surrounded. For

this reason he wanted to immigrate to Medina like his friends as soon as possible. However, he needed to return the deposits entrusted to him back to their owners.

The Prophet was the most reliable of all people. Everybody trusted him, so they would always entrust their precious things to him. Meccans had been doing this long before he became a prophet, too.

The Prophet prepared for his journey. If he had done it himself, it would have taken a long time to return the deposits to their owners. He thought that the best solution was to leave them with a reliable person. His cousin Ali ibn Abi Talib could do it for him. He sent a message to Ali. He had always been with the Prophet since he was a very little young boy. He accepted Islam at a very young age. He had never left the Prophet even in very hard times. When he heard that the Prophet called him, he went to him right away.

The Prophet was getting ready. "I'm going to go to Medina," he said to Ali.

Then he showed the deposits and told him what belonged to whom. He asked Ali to stay in his house, sleep in his bed that night, and then to return the deposits back to their owners the next day.

Ali accepted the Prophet's proposal. He was going to sleep in the Prophet's bed that night, so that the people outside the house would think the Prophet was at home.

Before he left home, the Prophet said to Ali:

"After finishing the tasks I asked you to do, get ready and come to Medina. I'll meet you there."

Ali loved the Prophet very much. He was always ready to do everything he said. He understood the importance of the task he was given by the Prophet. He was not scared at all.

The sun had set; it was dark everywhere. A group of polytheists gathered in front of the doors and the windows of the houses around the Prophet's house. They all had sharp swords. They thought they had a foolproof plan.

The Prophet prayed to God and then took a handful of soil from the ground. He opened the door and threw the soil towards the polytheists waiting outside, reciting the verse: "And We have set a barrier before them and a barrier behind them, and (thus) We have covered them (from all sides), so that they cannot see..." (Ya-Sin, 36:9) and walked away. God protected the Prophet. They could not see him, which was a miracle of God, so they remained in position, waiting for him to leave.

Although they had waited for many hours, nobody left the house. They started to get impatient.

"I don't think he is going to leave," one of them said.

"He will have to leave sooner or later! He can't stay in there forever!" said another one.

They continued to wait. They waited and waited. After a very long time, they almost lost their hope that the door would open.

While they were waiting around the Prophet's house, someone saw them.

"Why are you waiting here?" he asked.

"We are waiting for Muhammad to come out of his house!" they replied.

The man was surprised by their answer. He had seen the Prophet a while ago while he was walking away from Mecca.

"But he can't be at home. I just saw him going somewhere," he said.

"Are you making fun of us? We've been waiting here since last night. We have surrounded his house. It would have been impossible for him to leave without being noticed by us," they said.

Of course, they didn't know that God always protected him. They

had never thought that someone could have gotten out without being seen by them.

"You are a liar! We are going to break in the house!" they said.

They kicked the door down. They drew their swords and entered the house. It was very quiet in the house. Assuming that the Prophet was sleeping, they went into the bedroom. Someone was sleeping in the bed. One of them whispered:

"Look over there! The man lied to us. Muhammad is sleeping in his bed."

Another man said:

"We've found him. He is still sleeping unaware that he is going to be killed in no time."

One of them pulled the blanket. They were all shocked to see someone else sleeping in the bed; it was Ali! They looked at each other. They didn't know what to do!

"Where is Muhammad?" they asked angrily.

The young hero Ali looked at them bravely.

"I don't know," he said

They left the home angrily.

Ali risked his life sleeping in the Prophet's bed. He knew that he could have been killed doing this, but he fulfilled his task without thinking about that. God protected him from the polytheists.

The men on the assassination team went back to see Abu Jahl and his friends.

Abu Jahl welcomed them happily.

"Here they come. They are going to bring us good news," he said.

He was surprised to see the expression on their faces, and he became angry when he learned what had happened. Their plan didn't work. They were all angry.

"Is Muhammad still alive? We've failed to get rid of him once again," they said.

Abu Jahl said:

"We are going to look for him. We will kill him wherever we find him."

They decided to go to Abu Bakr's house, the Prophet's's closest friend, first. They didn't find him at home either because the Prophet and Abu Bakr had already left for Medina together. The next day Ali gave the things that the Prophet entrusted to him back to their owners, and then he prepared to go to Medina.

THE VALUE OF ALMS

The grandsons of the Prophet, Hasan and Husayn, loved to go walking around the city with their father Ali. They were very young. When their father was free, they would often go out for a walk together. They would hold each other's hands and see the most beautiful places of Medina.

One day, they went out for a walk as usual. While they were walking in the street, an old man came up to them. The man, who looked exhausted, said:

"I am very hungry. I couldn't find anything to eat today. Would you please help me?"

The old man looked very poor and miserable. His clothes were very old and torn. After listening to him, Ali said to himself: "I should help this man. He really needs help."

He searched through his pockets. He wanted to give him some money. When the old man saw Ali searching through his pockets, he felt very happy and hopeful.

Hasan and Husayn were watching the old man. They felt sorry for the poor man too.

Ali searched through his pockets, but he couldn't find any money. Then he remembered that he gave all his money to his wife Fatima before he left home.

"The man felt so hopeful when he saw me searching through my pockets. I shouldn't disappoint him," he thought.

"I am sorry but I didn't take any money with me. If you could wait for some time, I will send my kids home to bring you some money," he said.

"Of course, I will," the poor man said with a shy and hoarse tone of voice.

Ali turned to his sons, who were watching what was going on carefully, and said:

"This morning, I gave your mom six drachmas. I want you to bring one of them to me."

Hasan and Husayn, who felt sorry for the poor man, were so willing to go home.

"OK, Daddy!" they said and headed for home.

They ran home and knocked at the door. Their mother Fatima was

very surprised when she opened the door because the kids left home with their father in the morning but returned alone.

Hasan and Husayn wanted to take the money as quickly as possible, so they didn't let her say or ask anything and said:

"Mom! Daddy wanted us to take him one of the six drachmas that he gave you this morning."

Fatima didn't know that her husband wanted the money to help a poor man, so she said:

"But we don't have any flour at home. Your father gave me this money to buy some flour. Maybe he forgot all about this. Go ask him if he changed his mind or not."

"OK Mommy! We will go and ask," they said and left.

Ali and the poor man were waiting for the kids to come back. Hasan and Husayn came running.

"Did you bring the money?" Ali asked.

"Daddy, Mom said that you had given her the money to buy some flour, and she wanted to know if you changed your mind or not," said Hasan.

Ali didn't want to disappoint the poor man.

"Go tell your mother I am going to use that money for something more important and bring all of the six drachmas I gave her," he said.

The boys went home running again and knocked on the door.

"What happened?" asked their mother asked curiously.

"Mom! Daddy wanted us to bring him all the money that he gave you. He said he was going to use it for something more important," the boys said.

Then Fatima brought the money from inside and gave it to them.

"Here is the money. But be careful, do not loose it. Okay?" she said.

The kids took the money to their father.

"Here you are, Daddy! We brought all of the money," said Hasan and gave the money to his father.

Ali took the money and gave it to the poor man. The poor man was very happy. He thanked them, prayed for them, and left.

Ali and his sons walked more for a while and then decided to go back home. When they arrived home, a man with a camel approached

and greeted them. After greeting him, Ali asked the man where he was going.

"I am going to the marketplace to sell this camel. If you want, I can sell it to you," the man said to Ali.

"How much do you ask for it?" Ali asked.

"One hundred and forty drachmas," the man replied.

That price was really low for such a big and beautiful camel. Ali thought for a short time and said,

"I would like to buy it, but I don't have any money right now. I can give you the money after a short while. If you agree, I will buy it," he said.

The man said:

"OK, it's a deal. I would never do this for someone else, but I know that you are a trustworthy person."

"Okay, then tie the camel's bridle to this tree in front of the house," Ali said.

The man tied the camel's halter. He said goodbye and left. Ali was standing in front of his house looking at the camel. A man who was passing by greeted him and said:

"What a pretty camel. I need one like this. Would you sell it to me?"

"Yes, I would," Ali said.

"How much do you want?"

"Two hundred drachmas."

The man accepted this price and gave Ali two hundred drachmas. He untied the camel and took it away.

Hasan and Husayn went inside their home. Ali went to find the other man whose camel he bought and gave him the money. Ali found the man after a long search and said:

"I came to you to give your money for the camel you sold me."

After leaving the market place, Ali went straight home. When he entered the home, he gave sixty drachmas to his wife. Fatima was really surprised to see that much money. "Where did you get this money"? she asked. That morning her husband had said "this is our last money." It was just six drachmas, which was one tenth of this money.

Ali explained the situation:

"God Almighty said to the Prophet 'Whoever does any good deed will be rewarded with ten times of it in return.' We gave those six drachmas to a poor man, and God sent us ten times of it in return. Our six drachmas returned to us as sixty drachmas."

THE LOST ARMOR

Ali, the fourth caliph of Muslims, was walking around in the marketplace. He was watching the behavior of the salesmen and the customers. He was talking with people and listening to their complaints. He talked to the salesmen and asked about their needs. Ali approached another seller to talk to him. There was armor on his counter among other products. He was really surprised. The armor that the seller was trying to sell was his armor. Ali had lost it a few days before, and he hadn't been able to find it yet. He was curious to know who this seller was.

Meanwhile, the man was shouting,

"Good armor for sale!"

Ali approached the man and said:

"This armor is mine - you can't sell it."

The man knew Ali, but he pretended not to know him.

"No, it is mine, and I want to sell it," he said:

Ali insisted on his claim and said:

"This armor is mine. I lost it a few days ago."

The people who heard the argument gather around them. They were trying to make out what was going on. Nobody liked the behavior of the seller to Ali because he was the caliph of Muslims. But they couldn't say anything since they didn't know exactly what had caused the argument.

The heated argument continued on.

"I am sure that it's mine. I know it from the sword marks on it," said Ali.

"Any armor may have these kinds of marks. You have to prove it that it is yours," the seller replied.

Ali picked up the armor. He checked it thoroughly. He was absolutely sure that it was his armor. How could he possibly forget the armor that he wore for every battle? But he didn't know how to prove it.

"Let's go to the court then," Ali said.

At first, the seller didn't want to accept Ali's offer. When he saw that everybody was staring at him sourly, he thought he had no other option and said:

"Okay. Let's go to the court."

Ali and the seller went to the court.

The seller said to the judge:

"I am not a Muslim. I am a Christian. I am afraid that your judgment will not be fair."

"Your religion is of no importance to me. I am going to decide in favor of the one who is right," said the judge.

The seller was still anxious even after he heard what the judge had just said. The man who sued him was the leader of Muslims, so he thought the judge would favor Ali.

The judge let Ali speak first.

"This armor is mine. I lost it a few days ago. I looked for it but I couldn't find it. Then I saw this man trying to sell it," said Ali.

The Christian seller asked for permission to speak.

"I asked him to prove his claim," he said.

The judge turned to Ali and asked:

"Do you have two witnesses who know that is your armor?"

"Yes, of course I do! If you allow me, I will bring them to you."

"Okay. Go get them," said the judge.

Ali left the court and went to find the witnesses. He was going to invite his son Hasan and his servant to the court. He went home hurriedly. Luckily both of them were at home.

"Get ready, we have to go!" he said.

Hasan and the servant were surprised because they didn't know where they were going.

When Hasan asked where they were going, Ali explained the situation.

It didn't take them long to get to the court. The judge knew Hasan, but he didn't know the man next to him. Pointing to the servant, he asked: "Who is this man?"

"He is my servant. He is one of the people who knows my belongings very well."

"Okay. Your servant can be a witness for you but your son Hasan cannot," said the judge.

Ali was very surprised to hear this.

"Why? Everybody knows that Hasan is a very reliable person. The Prophet praised him," said Ali.

"I know that Hasan is a very reliable person. I myself heard the Prophet praising him," replied the judge.

When judge said those things everybody thought that he was going to accept him as a witness. But he turned to Ali and said:

"However, a father and a son cannot testify as a witness for each other according to Islamic law. Could you please find another witness instead of Hasan?"

Meanwhile, the seller was watching everything in great surprise. When he first came to the court, he had thought, "I am a Christian, and they are Muslims. And Ali is the caliph of Muslims. How could a judge possibly be impartial in such a trial?"

But the judge never wavered in his impartial perspective. He treated him as if he wasn't a caliph but an ordinary person in the court. The judge could try a caliph and also refuse his witness. The seller was lost in amazement. He turned to judge and said:

"Stop!"

Everybody was curious about what he was going to say!

"One day the caliph Ali was riding his camel, and I was walking behind him. His armor fell down, but he wasn't aware of this. I took it, and a few days later, I took it to the marketplace to sell it. But now I regret having done such a bad thing. Yes, this armor belongs to Ali," said the seller.

The seller was really moved. He continued:

"I understand that Islam is a great religion. Muslims are really trustworthy people. Even the caliph of Muslims can't get his own property back from person with a different religion as he wishes. The judge did not accept even the caliph's son as a witness. I want to convert to such a great religion; I want to become a Muslim, too."

After his moving speech, he became a Muslim by saying "There is no deity but God, and Muhammad is the Messenger of God."

Ali was very pleased to see that the seller became a Muslim. He hugged and congratulated him. He picked up the armor from the floor and said:

"Please take this armor, and I also want to give you a horse as a gift."

Everybody was smiling as they were leaving the court.